The Buddha

sacred symbols

The Buddha

294.3
BUD

Thames and Hudson

THE THREE JEWELS

$\mathbf{T}$*he 2500-year history of Buddhism has seen its beliefs, rituals and symbolism gradually spread from its birthplace in India to Tibet, Nepal, the countries of south-east Asia, and Japan. Unlike other major religions, Buddhism*

does not have a draconian deity at its head, but rather places the responsibility for salvation in the hands of its disciples, both lay and ordained. The latter, the monastic communities, occupy a central position in the Buddhist world; in their practices, in their art and architecture, we shall find the most complex symbolism associated with the Buddha. But because of the very openness of this tolerant and accommodating religion, the symbolism itself is subtle and wide-ranging. Much of it concerns the Buddha himself, his life and representations, his doctrine (dharma) *and the community of Buddhists* (sangha), *known as 'The Three Jewels'. The Buddha saw his life and teaching in terms of this triad – hence the divisions of this book.*

Opposite The Buddha descending from a mountain after preaching (ink painting, China, *c.* 14th century).

These Three Jewels constitute the world of the Buddhist. The representations of the Buddha, for instance, can indicate many things — meditation, teaching, Enlightenment or death, according to attitude or posture; even the Buddha's feet have their own particular significance.

The dharma, *the doctrine of the Buddha based on his formulation of the Four Noble Truths, is itself symbolized by the wheel, while other symbols — the path, for example — crystallize for the initiate the*

way in which the teachings must be applied. Those who follow the dharma *constitute the* sangha, *the community of Buddhists in its wider sense, but more usually applied strictly to the monastic order which ensures the survival of the* dharma *and lives a life of devotion to the original values taught by the Buddha. These values are made manifest in both secular and monastic life by an elaborate system of symbols.*

The Three Jewels: the Buddha, with begging bowl, and figures of monks, the *sangha*, by which humanity participates in the *dharma* (detail from *tanka*, Tibet, 19th century).

THE BUDDHA

The ways of representing the figure of the Buddha through the ages often reflect the stages of his life and his teaching. Born about 566 B.C. in Nepalese Terai to parents of the Sakya tribe, he was later known as Sakyamuni, or 'sage of the Sakya tribe', or as Gautama, his clan name. He also referred to himself as Tathagata, or 'one who follows in the path of his predecessors', although his own forename was Siddhartha, meaning 'aim attained'. Later worshippers came to know him through images and symbols which reflected the episodes of his life and his meditation techniques.

Queen Maya gives birth to the Buddha through her right side in this Tibetan painting.

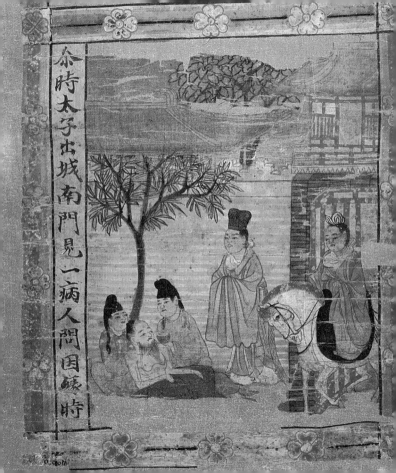

余時太子出城南門見一病人悶困羸時

the three marks

the first significant event in the adult life of Gautama was his encounter with the Three Marks of Impermanence: old age, illness and death. After a life of relative ease, during which he married and had a son and lived under the protection of his father, the Buddha strayed beyond the normal confines of the family grounds and there encountered three sights which were to transform his life: an old man, crippled by age; the second, a man riddled with disease; the third, a corpse borne on its final journey to the cremation ground. Such was the young man's sense of suffering that he decided to seek true salvation.

The Buddha is said to have been told by the women of his household of the beauty of the woods beyond the house. These revelations made him especially anxious to see life beyond the confines of his family.

Opposite The life of the young Buddha: the encounters with the aged man and the sick man (silk painting, China, 8th or early 9th century A.D.).

enlightenment

The Buddha was especially critical of both those who placed a premium on the world of the senses and of those who deliberately tormented themselves as ways to salvation.

a*fter failing to reach complete spiritual satisfaction through a regime of unremitting asceticism and ardent study of the teachings of others, the Buddha continued his wanderings. Eventually he found himself in Bodh-Gaya, and there, sheltered by an ancient fig tree, he gave himself up to transcendental meditation for forty-nine days before attaining total Enlightenment.*

Opposite The Buddha touches the earth with his right hand, the posture of Enlightenment (detail from silk painting, China, *c.* A.D. 900).

The Buddha sets in motion the wheel of the *dharma*
(relief, Afghanistan, 5th century A.D.).

gods are divided into five main groups, each
under one of five celestial Buddhas and each
divided into quarters. This five/four symbolism
is extended to make the great cosmic diagrams
in the form of mandalas. The Buddha's
universality was celebrated in the legend that he
could assume a thousand forms.

bodhisattvas

literally 'enlightened being', from sattva, *'being' or 'essence', and* bodhi, *the wisdom arising from the realization of the ultimate truth, the bodhisattva played a crucial role in Mahayana Buddhism. The ideal of the bodhisattva was to renounce* nirvana *in order to help all other beings to salvation. These figures are often shown richly attired, emphasizing their worldliness in contrast to the simplicity of the Buddha. Important bodhisattvas: Maitreya, the Buddha to be, is crowned by a* stupa; *Vajrapani holds a thunderbolt; Avalokiteshvara protects travellers.*

Nagarjuna described a bodhisattva as someone destined to become a Buddha.

Opposite The bodhisattva Avalokiteshvara as a guide (ink and colours on silk, China, 10th century A.D.).

goddesses

female deities had traditionally acted as symbols of fertility in early Indian religion. In Buddhism such figures were known as yakshas. The growth of Tantric and esoteric Buddhism saw a considerable increase in the number and complexity of female figures. Some of these were multi-limbed monsters, expressive of great evil, while others symbolized wisdom and were presented in passive, beatific postures.

The meaning of the goddess Tara is one of the hardest to unravel in the Tibetan Buddhist pantheon; she has as many heads and legs as she has arms, a complex arrangement which may account for the rarity of such sculptures.

Opposite Tara is Avalokiteshvara's female counterpart; she is the scourge of humans, birds and animals. The two cubes beneath her feet symbolize egocentric existence (partly gilt brass, Tibeto-Chinese, 18th century).

DHARMA

After achieving Enlightenment under the *bodhi* tree, the Buddha continued his meditations, formulating a doctrine which could then be passed on to others. This doctrine became known as the *dharma*, meaning 'law' or 'teaching'. It was said to have first been recited after the death of the Buddha by Ananda, the favourite disciple, and it then became the guiding principle for the whole community of Buddhists. Central to the doctrine are the Four Noble Truths, though the teaching of Buddhism has never been rigid and doctrinaire; it has always adapted to circumstances. Certain symbols and emblems, however, retain enduring significance, such as the wheel and the path.

Opposite The translation of Buddhist scripture into Tibetan: here the translator, watched over by Buddhas and bodhisattvas, hands down leaves to copying scribes (*tanka*, Tibet, 18th century).

the four noble truths

EVERYTHING IS SUFFERING

THE ORIGIN OF SUFFERING IS DESIRE

THERE EXISTS NIRVANA, AN END TO SUFFERING

A PATH, DEFINED BY THE BUDDHA, LEADS TO NIRVANA.

Opposite The Wheel of Life illustrates the chain of dependent origination, one of the most important concepts of Buddhist doctrine (gouache on cloth, Tibet, 18th century).

These four Truths were the central points of the Buddha's doctrine. The first refers to the unsatisfactory nature of life, its impermanence. Our belief in selfhood is the second Truth: Self has five components or skandhas – Matter, Sensations, Perceptions, Mental Formations and Consciousness. Nirvana is the end of suffering, the abandonment of selfhood. Finally, there is 'The Noble Eightfold Path': Right Understanding, Right Thought, Right Speech, Right Action, Right Livelihood, Right Effort, Right Mindfulness and Right Meditation.

the wheel

from earliest times Buddhist art was characterized by rich symbolism, often derived from the circumstances of the Buddha's first teachings. Images of trees, thrones and wheels were especially significant. The wheel was an emblem of the dharma, the setting in motion of the wheel of law, and therefore a symbol of the Buddha himself. It could also be symbolized by the circle formed by bringing the tips of thumb and forefinger together, signifying the perfection which is neither beginning nor end.

Opposite Symbol of the *dharma*, the wheel became one of the most elaborately worked symbols of Buddhist iconography (low-relief sculpture in silver-gilt, copper and semi-precious stones, Tibet, 19th century).

the path

The fourth Noble Truth of the Buddha's doctrine refers to the path towards Enlightenment, nirvana. Later teaching divided the path by stages – from morality to meditation, and then to wisdom. The Buddha, however, recognized that wholehearted commitment to following the path was virtually impossible for anyone living in the world of normal human exchange and therefore propounded his doctrine of the 'Middle Way' between luxury and asceticism. Meditation walks, terminating in a shelter housing the image of a skeleton, are still used by monks in Sri Lanka to represent the path of earthly life.

Opposite The path to Enlightenment is graphically illustrated by the progression of elephants in this mural from the monastery of Likir, Ladakh.

The Buddha, quoted by Ashvaghosha in the *Buddhacarita,* saw the way to supreme Enlightenment as a path trodden for the sake of all that is sad in the world.

the bodhi tree

this central symbol in Buddhist iconography represents the original fig tree which sheltered the Buddha during the extraordinary night of his Enlightenment. In early Buddhist art the figure of the Buddha in the Enlightenment posture was often shown with cuttings from the fig tree, later stylized as the royal parasol, symbol of the shelter given him by the tree during his night of liberation. Cuttings from the fig tree were taken to bless any new site devoted to the religion. In later, more elaborate monastic structures, the tree was symbolized in the crowning finial of the stupa.

Opposite Painting on a leaf showing a monkey offering a peach (symbol of sexual enjoyment) to a devotee beneath a *bodhi* tree (China, 19th century).

posture

Buddhist statuary is characterized by postures of great physical gracefulness, as in this figure of a listening disciple (Burma, 19th century).

Just as representations of the Buddha show him in various postures to symbolize certain states – meditation, Enlightenment, leadership, and death – so posture and position are used as aids to the successful negotiating of the path to Enlightenment. Buddhist statuary almost always suggests grace and ease, as though expressing the spirituality of the subject. In Zen Buddhism the process of awakening is helped by the technique of zazen, in which the initiate sits cross-legged in the lotus position and brings his mind to a state of peace and tranquillity by slow, rhythmic breathing.

Opposite A more regal figure is this bodhisattva (polychromed wood, China, 12th–13th century).

in the deer park

EVERYTHING IS SUFFERING

THE ORIGIN OF SUFFERING IS DESIRE

THERE EXISTS NIRVANA, AN END TO SUFFERING

A PATH, DEFINED BY THE BUDDHA, LEADS TO NIRVANA.

during the period before his Enlightenment beneath the fig tree, five mendicants accompanied the Buddha and witnessed his efforts to achieve the highest spiritual knowledge through asceticism. After his abandonment of that path, the five left him and repaired to the Deer Park near Benares, to which the Buddha returned after Enlightenment. There, he delivered the discourse 'The Setting in Motion of the Wheel of the Doctrine', in which he laid down the Four Noble Truths.

Overleaf
The Buddha preaching to his disciples (illuminated manuscript, Burma, 19th century).

death of the buddha

the death of Shakyamuni was no ordinary death, but rather another turn in the cycle of rebirth and suffering. It was at the age of eighty that the Buddha, accompanied by his preferred follower Ananda and other disciples, was finally overtaken by illness. Reclining between two trees in the forest of Uparavarta near Kusinagara, he addressed his faithful band, urging them to work towards their own Enlightenment, but refusing to pronounce on what happens to an enlightened person after death, since that is beyond human thought and expression.

Opposite The dying Buddha reclining between the two trees of Kusinagara (*tanka*, Tibet, late 19th or early 20th century).

When the Buddha reached Kusinagara, he ordered Ananda to prepare a couch for him, announcing that this was the night that he, Tathagata, would enter *nirvana*.

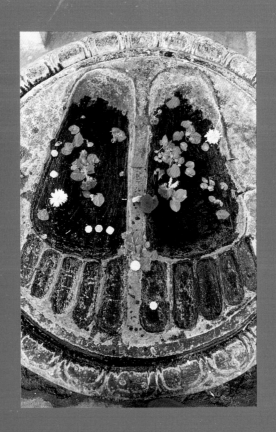

images of the buddha

about five hundred years after the death of the Buddha there began to emerge a new school of Buddhism, the Mahayana, which concentrated on the more abstract, celestial aspects of the teacher's power,

After his death, the relics of the Buddha were the object of veneration and worship. Ambassadors were even sent from seven neighbouring kingdoms to ask for parts of them.

in contrast to the Theravada, the 'path of the elders', which sought inspiration in the episodes of the Buddha's life on earth. Hence, the representation of the Buddha in Mahayana art, prevalent in northern Asia, tended to be as a transcendent being. The soles of the Buddha's feet and his footprints were also venerated, symbolizing the grounding of the transcendent and its application to the present.

Opposite Offerings of petals and coins on a representation of the Buddha's footprints adjacent to the Mahabodhi Temple, Bodh-Gaya.

the buddha crowned

the images of the Buddha have, through the ages, been attended by special attributes: cranial enlargement, to indicate superior mental and spiritual powers, for example, or curled and tufted hair. The Mahayana view of the regal, celestial status of the Buddha inspired some notable images, including the crowned Buddha and the arms-raised Buddha as world ruler. The first examples of the crowned figure occurred after the 7th century A.D. in India, and were then taken up in Central Asia where the Mahayana school was especially well-established and much taken by the regal aspects of the sage.

According to the *Mahaprajnaparamitashastra* of Nagarjuna, who lived in the 2nd century A.D., there can be only one single universal monarch in any Four-Continent system.

The Buddha crowned – the image for those disciples of purified minds (copper alloy gilded, China, early 15th century).

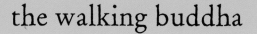

the walking buddha

this highly stylized way of representing the Buddha was closely associated with the ancient Thai capital of Sukhotai. It was characterized especially by a peculiar grace in the proportions and suggested movement of the Buddha — symbolizing, perhaps, the final harmony achieved in his life. Most standing Buddhas from other parts of Asia convey the act of walking only by the position of the head, but the images from Sukhotai show the Buddha striding forward, though with great balance and elegance, reminding Buddhists, perhaps, of the peripatetic, mendicant origins of the faith.

A rare image of the Buddha actually walking (bronze, Sukhotai, Thailand, 14th century).

Every aspect of
physical movement –
sitting, standing still,
walking – should
be a matter for
careful consideration,
according to
Ashvaghosha, a poet
of the 1st or 2nd
century A.D.

The Buddha in
graceful movement
against the
background of
his throne (bronze,
India, 6–7th
century A.D.).

the seated buddha

the image of the Buddha seated is the one which most suggests peace in a turbulent world. It is one, too, which is particularly appropriate to worship, although each separate effigy needs to acquire spiritual significance through consecration rituals before it becomes powerful enough to be the recipient of prayer. The image, too, once thus rendered meaningful, may also act as an inspiration to meditation in the way a mandala gives the devotee a guiding structure for spiritual reflection. Seated Buddhas in the meditation or Enlightenment postures are sometimes surmounted by a parasol, symbol of the fig tree which sheltered Shakyamuni when he achieved nirvana.

According to Buddhist tradition, the great sage is always represented sitting under the tree as he makes his vow to seek Enlightenment.

Opposite Hands in the discussion position, this Buddha is seated on a lotus, symbol of his teaching (ink on paper, China, 10th century A.D.).

the meditating buddha

Ashvaghosha's writings on meditation advocate sitting cross-legged, preferably in a lonely place, and concentrating on the tip of the nose or the space between the eyebrows.

Opposite The Buddha in the meditation posture (gilt statue, Sukhotai, Thailand, 14th century).

During the night under the fig tree the Buddha eventually gained Enlightenment through meditation: on his former lives, on the birth and death of beings, and on the ignorance which had held him bound to this world and to the constant necessity of rebirth. In representations of the Buddha, especially in south-east Asia, we find the meditation posture constantly recurring. The Buddha is characteristically in a squatting position, hands clasped in front of the body, with an expression of supreme calm. In such images he is often shown protected by a parasol, symbol of the fig tree at Bodh-Gaya.

the celestial cosmic buddha

the Mahayana school of Buddhism, which emerged about five hundred years after the death of Shakyamuni, placed fresh emphasis on the whole pantheon of Buddhas and bodhisattvas. This emphasis is even more striking in esoteric Buddhism – Indian and Tibetan Tantrism, for instance – where the

This scroll (*below*), depicting a series of Buddhas under different names, was used in ceremonies on the last day of the lunar year (ink and colours on paper, China, 10th century).

hands

In Buddhism, as in Hinduism, movements of the hands are seen to symbolize movements of the mind and, as such, are central to expressing the meaning of the dharma. Many of these hand gestures (mudra) may be observed in representations of the Buddha. To the initiate the vocabulary is very clear: thumb and forefinger closed recall the wheel, and therefore the dharma itself; the hands upright and open signify the teaching of the doctrine; the open hand pointing downwards is the gesture of generosity and giving; hands folded on the lap indicate meditation.

Opposite The hands of a monk in the wheel gesture, Eiheiji, Japan.

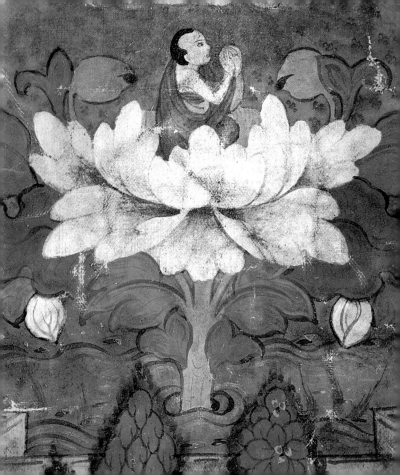

lotus

Spiritual purity, **bodhi**, is symbolized especially by the eight-petalled white lotus, the lotus of the Buddha.

Opposite This lotus, symbol of the *dharma*, rises up to the heavens to support the figure of a monk, symbol of the *sangha* (detail from *tanka*, Tibet, 19th century).

The aquatic lotus was an ideal symbol of Enlightenment: its roots were in muddy waters, representative of human desires, while the leaves and flowers opened up to the sun, to Enlightenment. Legends of the Buddha's birth and first days tell how the infant caused a lotus to spring up every time his foot touched the ground as he took his first steps. The opening of the lotus also symbolizes the opening of the chakras, the nerve centres of the body.

mandala

Opposite Mandala with Buddha and bodhisattvas (ink on silk, Japan, c. A.D. 859–880).

A mandala can assume any size: the greatest one in the world is the temple complex of Borobudur, Java, a colossal edifice of concentric terraces and *stupas*.

As an aid to spiritual fulfilment and, therefore, to progress along the path to Enlightenment, the mandala is a central emblem of Buddhism. Its circular form, with neither beginning nor end, and concentric structure reflect the shape of the universe outside and the sense of perfection within. Buddhist mandalas guide meditation and prayer and also often reflect the forms of the cosmos. At the centre of the universe is Mount Meru, surrounded by seven concentric mountain ranges separated by the seven oceans. Beyond the outermost range lie the great ocean and the four island continents, including the southernmost, Jambudvipa, the home of humans. In the heights of Mount Meru live the four Buddhas of the cardinal points and, at its peak, the celestial Buddha, Vairochana.

meditation

*the Buddha taught that the way to
Enlightenment is through meditation and the
achievement of a calm, clear state of being,
mirroring his own experience under the* bodhi
*tree. This discipline of constructive thought will
enable the disciple to rise above the three forces
of ignorance, desire and hatred* (samsara),
*symbolized by the pig, cock and snake.
In Zen Buddhism the meditation discipline
of* zazen *has two characteristics: stopping*
(shi) *and view* (kan).

Opposite A monk
of a Japanese
Buddhist sect sits in
meditation beneath
a tree, savouring the
delights of nature as
an aid to gaining
true spirituality
(Japan, 12th–13th
century).

light

the light of the world rising up through the chakras *leads to the supreme Enlightenment. Light is everywhere in the universe in various shades and intensities and is therefore a symbol of the ultimate reality and always one of the main offerings at Buddhist shrines. In Thailand this may take the form of an orange candle combined with flowers and three sticks of sandalwood. The first symbolizes individual consciousness; the second, the senses; and the third, the tripartite division of Buddhism, the 'Three Jewels' of Buddha,* dharma *and* sangha. *Valuable materials, such as butter, are used to make candles, signifying the importance of the offering.*

In Buddhism light is especially associated with the positive aspects of life after death, guiding the departed one to various worlds of delight.

Opposite Butter lamps (Dharamsala, India).

water

A tranquil lake is a metaphor in Zen for a mind which has become pure and calm through meditation.

like the light of the candle, water is a frequent symbolic offering at Buddhist shrines and temples. It is closely associated with the symbolism of the moon as an image of the feminine, regenerative power in the universe. On special occasions and for particular deities the water may be further purified by the addition of herbs. Contemplation of water, whether still or falling, is also regarded as an aid to meditation; in Zen Buddhism, especially, the initiate will go through several levels of consciousness to reach a true appreciation of the very essence of the substance.

Water has long been recognized as an aid to meditation; here, in this Chinese temple (*opposite*), its tranquillity makes an apt setting for the symbolic *stupa*.

the serpent

The Buddha is sheltered here (*opposite*) by the serpent-being Muchalinda, who had protected him during a storm in the garden at Bodh-Gaya (Cambodia, 12th century).

Ashvaghosha described the cross-legged posture adopted by the Buddha in meditation as making the legs 'massive like the coils of a sleeping serpent'.

The serpent Kundalini in Tantric symbolism represents the force rising up through the body, opening up the chakras until it reaches the seventh chakra of the 'thousand-petalled' lotus, positioned just above the head. Always an object of veneration in the animistic cultures of south-east Asia, the serpent was assimilated into the body of Buddhist belief as a protective presence, especially of the teachings and temples. As water symbols, serpents were seen as links between heaven and earth and often appeared as sculptural decoration in temple architecture to symbolize the passage from one state to another — on bridges over water or at entrances to temple complexes.

SANGHA

The third jewel of Buddhist belief is the *sangha* – the community of those who have accepted the tenets of the *dharma*. In its broadest sense the *sangha* is four-fold, including monks, nuns, laymen and laywomen; the former two categories are distinguished from the latter by dress, way of life, and intensity of spiritual application. All members of the *sangha* aspire to Enlightenment, as taught by the Buddha.

Left Marble statue of a monk with begging bowl (Burma, 19th century); villagers, however poor, are expected to help sustain Buddhist communities by giving to the monks (*opposite*) (illuminated manuscript, Thailand, 19th century).

pillars

Visual symbolism in the holy places of
Buddhism only began to appear
approximately three hundred years after
the Buddha's death. In northern India,
the Emperor Ashoka (ruled c. 272–231
B.C.), a convert to Buddhism, took over
the practice of pillar worship from earlier
Indian cults to promote the spread of
Buddhism. Pillars in stone and wood,
carved with the sayings of the Buddha
and surmounted by symbolic beasts, were
set up throughout the empire, from Bengal
to Afghanistan, recalling the memorial
columns of Mesopotamia.

The most famous pillar of Ashoka is the lion
in polished sandstone at Sarnath, India (*left*).

stupa

After the relics of the Buddha had been dispersed to various kingdoms, the rulers there erected *stupas* in their principal cities to house them.

The best known of all Buddhist monuments, the stupa *is formed of a dome with a pillar emerging from its top. It is a simple icon of the Buddha's conquest of the world of illusion and his attainment of* nirvana. *The pillar itself represents the* axis mundi, *the pivotal point of the earth, the mystical Mount Meru, and is often enclosed by three umbrellas, symbolizing the Three Jewels. Circumambulation of the* stupa *is seen as an aid to meditation.*

Overleaf
a Nepalese monastery consisting of just four cells and *stupa* (illuminated manuscript, Nepal, A.D. 1015).

साभनदल
नवागनाग
।मजुवम शा
वागनावामे
आङनावाए
ग्राङ्क्षिवा
शावीष्द्र्वग

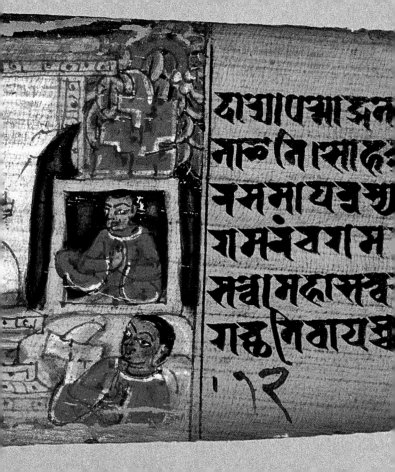

दाशाएआ ने
माल नि साह
नसमायवश्य
यमचंचराम
सव्वामहृसव
गाह निवाय चैं
१२

temple of the universe

buddhist temples are themselves symbols of great complexity. They are, in effect, four-dimensional maps of the universe according to the Buddhist cosmology. In Thai temples, for instance, there is a dominating central tower, a reference to Mount Meru, the sacred mountain and central axis of the cosmos, from which other elements of the complex are laid out according to the cardinal directions. The domed form of the stupa has a symbolic role in both time and space as a reference to the Cosmic Egg, the origin of the universe. Indeed, every level of the stupa is rich in symbolism: the base, dome, spire, capital and finial are associated with, respectively, earth, water, fire, air and ether — the five elements.

Opposite Samye, the oldest Buddhist teaching monastery in Tibet, a symbolic model of the cosmos built on the diagram of the mandala (gouache on a cotton *tanka*, Tibet, 18th–19th century).

shrines and sanctuaries

As expressions of the monastic, meditational aspects of Buddhism, sanctuaries and pilgrim shrines were associated with the very early periods of religion. The need for peace and quiet for constructive reflection gave such plans a central role, both practical and symbolic, in the development of Buddhism. Particularly notable are the rock sanctuaries of western India, often embellished with wood, a reminder of the early days spent by the Buddha and his followers in the forest. Pilgrims gather in temple relic stupas for worship.

Ashvaghosha in the *Saundaranandakavya* prophesies a longer life, strength and the ability to eliminate faults as the results of solitary meditation.

Shrines and holy places were sometimes taken over from local religions; this fourteenth-century Shinto mandala (*opposite*) from Kumano shows the gods as Buddhas and bodhisattvas. Monks' cells (*left*) are also regarded as places of intense spirituality.

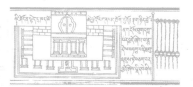

entrances

As holy buildings, especially those containing images of the Buddha, are symbols of the highest spiritual attainment, so the entrances to them are of especial significance. Symbols of the transition to a higher plane of being, temples and stupas are often embellished with massively elaborate decoration, emphasizing the importance to the initiate of the act of entering the shrine. Doors, too, may be richly carved, reflecting to the outside world the intensely sacred nature of the shrine's interior. The theme of passing from exterior to interior and vice versa is taken up again in bridges and their balustrades.

Opposite In the cave temples of Ellora in northern Deccan, India, bodhisattvas guard the preaching Buddha in a doorway carved in solid rock.

teacher and pupil

Just as entrances and bridges symbolize the passing from one spiritual state to another, so the relationship of teacher and pupil within the sangha is one in which the changing states of consciousness are of paramount importance. Although there are certain communal activities which give structure to monastery life, it is the passing on of spiritual knowledge – meditation techniques and an appreciation of the higher wisdoms – which ensures the continuing vigour of the religion. Every detail of a monk's life is redolent with symbolic meaning, and deviation from the daily round will entail a penance.

The Buddhist monk should struggle day and night to a point where he feels no weariness; then he will be ready to achieve *nirvana*.

An aged monk imparts wisdom to his pupils under the benevolent eye of a celestial being (wall painting, China, 9th–10th century).

'And so to the pleasant sound which issues from the water of these rivers, that reaches all the parts of this Buddha-field. And everyone hears the pleasant sound he wishes to hear, i.e. he hears of the Buddha, the *dharma*, the *sangha*...'
Sukhavaturjuba.

An offering of music, a medium reflecting the deepest rhythms of the universe – a graceful goddess depicted in a fresco in the temple of Drepung, Lhasa.

nirvana

all the symbolism
associated with the
sangha *is devoted to
one goal – the achievement
of a state of tranquillity beyond Self and the
physical sense. The making of music and the
intoning of mantras is seen as one of many
ways of aiding communication with the gods,
themselves sometimes symbolized as centres of
subtle sound, and of awakening the* chakras,
*the nerve centres of the body. Other activities
– gardening, writing, flower arranging, for
example – also help the devoted aspirant to
concentrate his mind towards spiritual
realization and the final silence which is
Enlightenment, the full assimilation of all the
symbolism of the Three Jewels.*

出 胎 圖

© 1996 Thames and Hudson Ltd, London

First published in the United States of America in 199[?] by Thames and Hudson Inc., 500 Fifth Avenue, New York, New York 10110

Library of Congress Catalog Card Number 95-61826

ISBN 0-500-06023-1

Printed and bound in Slovenia